First World War
and Army of Occupation
War Diary
France, Belgium and Germany

21 DIVISION
63 Infantry Brigade
Prince Albert's (Somerset Light Infantry)
8th Battalion
9 September 1915 - 31 July 1916

WO95/2158/3

The Naval & Military Press Ltd
www.nmarchive.com
Published in association with The National Archives

Published by

The Naval & Military Press Ltd

Unit 10 Ridgewood Industrial Park,

Uckfield, East Sussex,

TN22 5QE England

Tel: +44 (0) 1825 749494

www.naval-military-press.com

www.nmarchive.com

This diary has been reprinted in facsimile from the original. Any imperfections are inevitably reproduced and the quality may fall short of modern type and cartographic standards.

© Crown Copyright
Images reproduced by permission of The National Archives, London, England, 2015.

Contents

Document type	Place/Title	Date From	Date To
Heading	WO95/2158/3		
Miscellaneous	21st Division 63rd Infy Bde 6th Bn Som. Lt Infy Sep 1916-Jly 1916. To 37 Div 63 Bde.		
Miscellaneous	63rd Inf. Bde. 21st Div. Battn. disembarked Havre from England 10.9.15 War Diary 8th Battn. The Somerset Light Infantry. September (9.9.15-2.10.15) 1915	09/09/1915	09/09/1915
Heading	War Diary		
War Diary	Havre	09/09/1915	09/09/1915
War Diary	Watten	12/09/1915	12/09/1915
War Diary	Bayenghem	12/09/1915	12/09/1915
War Diary	Wardrecques	20/09/1915	20/09/1915
War Diary	Bourecq	21/09/1915	21/09/1915
War Diary	Ferfay	22/09/1915	22/09/1915
War Diary	Noeux Les Mines	24/09/1915	24/09/1915
War Diary	Vermelles	25/09/1915	25/09/1915
War Diary	Hulluch-Lens Road	26/09/1915	26/09/1915
War Diary	Hill 70		
War Diary	Vermelles	28/09/1915	28/09/1915
War Diary	Estree Blanche	01/10/1915	01/10/1915
War Diary	Steenbecque	02/10/1915	02/10/1915
War Diary	Borre	02/10/1915	02/10/1915
Heading	Report On Operation 25th/27th September.		
Miscellaneous	Report On Operations 25th 26th & 27th September	29/09/1915	29/09/1915
Heading	21st Division 63rd Inf Brigade. 8th Somerset L.I. Vol 2 Oct 15		
War Diary	Borre	02/10/1915	12/10/1915
War Diary	Strazeele	15/10/1915	24/10/1915
War Diary	Armentieres	25/10/1915	25/10/1915
Miscellaneous	Appendix 1		
Miscellaneous	C Form (Duplicate). Messages And Signals. Appendix II		
Miscellaneous	21st Division 8th Somerset L.I. Vol 3 Nov 15		
War Diary	Armentieres	01/11/1915	30/11/1915
Miscellaneous	App 1		
Miscellaneous	App 2		
Heading	21st Div 8th Som. L.I. Vol 4 December 1915		
War Diary	Armentieres	01/12/1915	24/12/1915
Miscellaneous	Battalion Operation Orders No. 13 by Lt. Col. L.C. Howard Commanding 8th (S) Battalion Somerset Light Infantry. App I	14/12/1915	14/12/1915
Miscellaneous	Report By Lieut. Shepherd R.E. In Charge of Party Which tried To Discover Mine Shaft on Night 15th/16		
Miscellaneous	Report on the Action of the Machine Guns During the minor Enterprise carried out on Nigh 15th/16th.		
Miscellaneous	Report On German Wire opposite the Mushroom.		
Miscellaneous	Report On A Minor Enterprise carried out by the 8th Somerset L.I., 63rd Infantry Brigade, 21st Division on the night of the 15th/16th December 1915	15/12/1915	15/12/1915
Map	Sketch to Illustrate Minor Enterprise on night of 15th 16th Dec 1915 Ref. Sheet 36		

Miscellaneous	2nd Army. G. 13		
Miscellaneous	Notes on Operation of December 15th/16th, 1915. 21st Divisional Artillery.	15/12/1915	15/12/1915
Miscellaneous	Account of an enterprise carried out on Second Army front on night of December 15th/16th.	27/12/1915	27/12/1915
Miscellaneous	Account of a Minor Operation carried out by 2nd Canadian Division on 15th December.	27/12/1915	27/12/1915
Miscellaneous	Report On minor Enterprise carried out 8th Bn. Somerset L.I., 63rd Infantry Brigade.		
Miscellaneous	Brigadier Orders By Brigadier General E.R. Hill, Commanding 63rd Infantry Brigade. App II	28/12/1915	28/12/1915
Heading	8th Som. L.I. Vol. 5 Jan 16		
War Diary	Armentieres	01/01/1916	25/02/1916
Miscellaneous	To Base Commandant E.A.D.	07/01/1916	07/01/1916
Miscellaneous	Appendix 1	10/02/1916	10/02/1916
Miscellaneous	Appendix 2	22/02/1916	22/02/1916
Heading	8 Somerset L.I. Vol 7		
War Diary	Armentieres	02/03/1916	20/03/1916
War Diary	Steenjte	20/03/1916	20/03/1916
War Diary	Strazeele	21/03/1916	01/04/1916
War Diary	Allonville	07/04/1916	07/04/1916
War Diary	Ville	07/04/1916	07/04/1916
War Diary	Meault	09/04/1916	23/04/1916
War Diary	Buire La Neuville	23/04/1916	30/04/1916
War Diary	La Neuville	02/05/1916	02/05/1916
War Diary	Buire	03/05/1916	15/05/1916
War Diary	La Neuville	22/05/1916	22/05/1916
Heading	War Diary Of 8th Somerset Light Infantry For June July 1916		
War Diary	La Neuville	02/06/1916	02/06/1916
War Diary	Ville	11/06/1916	15/06/1916
War Diary	La Neuville	20/06/1916	26/06/1916
War Diary	Ville	27/06/1916	27/06/1916
War Diary	Trenches	28/06/1916	02/07/1916
War Diary	Night of	02/03/1916	02/03/1916
War Diary	Lozenge Alley	03/07/1916	03/07/1916
War Diary	Ailly Sur Somme	04/07/1916	04/07/1916
War Diary	Bertangles	05/07/1916	06/07/1916
War Diary	Talmas	07/07/1916	07/07/1916
War Diary	Halloy	08/07/1916	10/07/1916
War Diary	Hannescamps Night	11/07/1916	31/07/1916

WO 2021/58113

21ST DIVISION
63RD INFY BDE

8TH BN SOM.LT INFY
SEP 1915-JLY 1916.

To 37 DIV 63 BDE

63rd Inf.Bde.
21st Div.

Battn. disembarked
Havre from England
10.9.15.

8th BATTN. THE SOMERSET LIGHT INFANTRY.

S E P T E M B E R
(9.9.15 - 2.10.15)

1 9 1 5

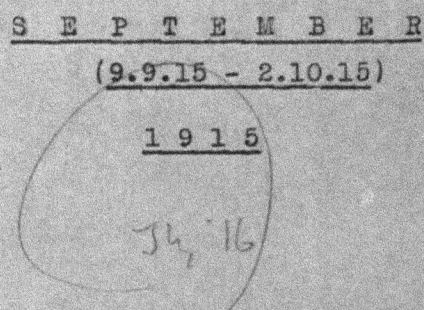

Attached:

Report on Operations
25th/27th September.

WAR DIARY.

Army Form C. 2118

WAR DIARY
~~INTELLIGENCE SUMMARY~~
(Erase heading not required.)

Instructions regarding War Diaries and Intelligence Summaries are contained in F. S. Regs., Part II. and the Staff Manual respectively. Title Pages will be prepared in manuscript.

Place	Date	Hour	Summary of Events and Information	Remarks and references to Appendices
HAVRE	9th September 1915		Left SOUTHAMPTON 9th September and arrived HAVRE morning of the 10th September. Spent	
WATTEN	12th Sep 1915		24 hours in Rest Camp then journeyed to WATTEN arriving WATTEN at 9 a.m. 12th September and from thence marched to BAYENGHEM arriving	
BAYENGHEM	12th Sep 1915		there about noon 12th September. We left BAYENGHEM about 8 p.m. 19th	
WARDRECQUES	20th Sep 15		September arriving WARDRECQUES on the 20th September, BOUREQ on the	
BOUREQ	21st Sep 15		21st September. FERFAY where we stayed two days on the 22nd September and	
FERFAY	22nd Sep		23rd Sep., FERFAY when we stayed two days on the 24th September. On the	
NOEUX LES MINES	24th Sep		bivouacked near NOEUX LES MINES on the 24th September.	
VERMELLES	25th Sep		morning of the 25th we marched to VERMELLES and deployed so into action about 7 p.m. on the 25th September. B and C Companies	
HULLUCH – LENS ROAD	26th Sep		went to the HULLUCH – LENS road held the road for the night of the 25th and on the morning of the 26th were counterattacked by the enemy and ordered to retire by the Brigade Major at 1 p.m. 26th Sep. They retired to the trenches and held them until 8 a.m. 27th Sep. when they marched to bivouac near VERMELLES and joined A and D Companies there. A and D Companies participated in an attack on HILL 70	
HILL 70	25 and 26th Sep		the night of 25 – 26th September and retired about 12 p.m. (m) on the 26th when they went into support lui del prernier trenches at VERMELLES were joined on the morning of the 27th Sep by B and C Companies. The Casualties in the Battalion numbered 15 Officers 271 other ranks. 13 mules and 1 horse. The Battalion stayed in bivouac	

Army Form C. 2118

WAR DIARY
INTELLIGENCE SUMMARY
(Erase heading not required.)

Instructions regarding War Diaries and Intelligence Summaries are contained in F. S. Regs., Part II. and the Staff Manual respectively. Title Pages will be prepared in manuscript.

Place	Date	Hour	Summary of Events and Information	Remarks and references to Appendices
VERMELLES	28th Sep.1915		near VERMELLES until the evening of the 28th when we marched to ESTREE BLANCHE stayed there until	
ESTREE BLANCHE	1st Oct.15			
STEENBECQUE	2nd Oct.15		1st October. marched to STEENBECQUE, left STEENBECQUE	
BORRE	2nd Oct.15		2nd October and arrived BORRE 2nd October where we now are.	

Borre.
2nd October 1915.

Atherley Colonel.
Commanding 8th Somerset L.I.

REPORT ON OPERATIONS 25TH/27TH
         SEPTEMBER.

A 16

REPORT ON OPERATIONS 25th 26th & 27th Septr. 1915

Reference Map
Sheet 36c 1/40000

by Maj Howard Som LI

Estree Blanche
29th September 1915

At 7 p.m. on the 25th September 1915, I received verbal orders to take "B" and "C" Companies 8th (S(Bn. Somerset L I as a firing line and go due EAST to make good the HULLUCH -Lens road at H 25 a. The 8th (S) Bn Lincoln Regiment were on my left. I started about 7 30 p.m. and about 9 45 p.m. I stopped for twenty minutes to make all my men fill their water-bottles and haversacks with water and provisions of which there was a good supply in our vacated first line trenches. I also sent back a messenger to ask Col. Denny who was bringing "A" and "D" Companies along as my supports to put out connecting files between the supports and me. The messenger broughtback word that the Adjutant did not think connecting files necessary. I then resumed the advance keeping close touch with the Lincolns on my left and arrived at my objective, the HULLUCH -LENS Road H25 a 8.7. at about 3 30 a.m. having searched the wood H25 a on my way. During the advance we were undr machine gun fire from the direction of H 25 d but had only two casualties

I then received orders from Brigadier General Nickalls to take up a position with one Company facing EAST along the HULLUCH-LNNS Road H 25 a 8.7. to H 25. and place the other company as Brigade reserve in the chalk pits at H25 a 7 7 . I placed "B" Company under Capt. Nichols along the HULLUCH-LENS road , but finding the Company too weak to hold so much line I asked for and obtained permission from Brig.Gen Nickalls to place another platoon there. This gave me 5 platoons along the HULLUCH-LENS road from H 25 a 8.7. to H 25 and three platoons in the chalk pits

(A and D Companies who had started out as my supports had gone astray and never found their way back to me) I made all hands spend the remainder of the night vigorously digging themselves in. From dawn onwards we were persistently sniped at but could not find the snipers At 8 20 a m I received orders for an advance on ANNAY and at 8 45 a m whilst reading and explaining these orders to my officers I was called for by the Brigade Major who informed me that we were being counter attacked on our right and asked me to place my three reserve platoons in position along the edge of the wood H 25 a facing S E. This I did finding them good natural cover and an old deserted shallow trench. A continuous heavy rifle fire was then opened upon us but I only had about three casualties as my men were well under cover. At about 9 20 a m Capt. Rose (the Staff Captain) came to me in an exhausted (winded) condition and asked me to send a messenger to the York and Lancaster Regiment who were on my right infront of wood H 25 a and tell them to send a company back to the trenches they had vacated along the HULLUCH -LENS road H 19c.

(1)

REPORT ON OPERATIONS 25th 26th & 27th Septr. 1915 (Con)

Nobody volunteered to go so I went myself and finding no officer in capable control I ordered about one hundred men back to their trenches and saw them safely in position there H.19.c. The Brigade Major asked me if I could spare a platoon to go there also. I sent Lieut. Marsh and his platoon there and spread out my men to take the place he had vacated. During this time a heavy rifle and machine gun fire was turned on us accompanied by a very heavy and accurate shell fire. However we were well entrenched and our casualties were remarkably few. At about 10 15 a m I saw the West Yorks who had been on my left front running back and shortly afterwards the Lincolns vacated their trenches and ran back also. (I could see a few men of both regiments were still left in the trenches however) The Germans now began to show their hand, coming out in the open from wood H 25 and 26 and attacking along my left front in a half hearted manner. The York and Lancs on my right had already retreated owing to the intensity of the enemy shell fire, so I drew in my right flank and made a redoubt of the CHALK-PITS The enemy then concentrated their fire on my position but without great effect - their shells going over our heads and bursting at the bottom of the CHALK PIT (see attached sketch). Their snipers were deadly though and 2nd Lt Hopkins was killed and Lt. Fitzmaurice wounded about this time A few minutes later 2nd Lt. Basker was killed. Earlier in the morning at the suggestion of the Brigade Major I had called for ten volunteers to bring ammunition. These men now returned with 2000 rounds saying it was all they could get. A few of my men whose officers had been killed had retreated whilst I was otherwise engaged. However, we were all in good spirits and blazed away at the Germans who were coming into full view all the time now. Captain Stromquist of the 8th Lincolns who had joined me earlier saying he could not find his Company was killed at about 11 a m

Things began to get warm now and we all took rifles and shot carefully along the wood wherever the enemy debouched, at ranges varying from 400 to 800 yards. Ammunition ran low so we stripped the dead of theirs and got enough to keep going and at 11.40 a m to our great joy we saw reinforcements (the attacking Brigade) coming over the brow of the slope behind us.

We shot freely now and held the Germans to their ground. Captain Nicholls was killed and Lt. Robinson wounded. At 12 30 p m reinforcements (the attacking brigade) reached our line "The Buffs" joining me at the CHALK PITS and bringing a very much needed machine gun with them which was very capably and pluckily handled by the machine gun officer. About 1 p m the attacking brigade retired and at 1 15 p m Major Macdonald (the Brigade Major) ordered me to retire because the attacking brigade in its retirement had left both both my flanks clear and because I had no ammunition left. I effected a retirement with very little loss, gathered together the men of the different regiments and manned the English front line trenches relieving Captain Wilson of the Highland Light Infantry. I remained there until 8 a m 27th September when I marched to bivouac.

Whilst at the CHALK PITS neither I nor any of my men saw or smelt any sign of gas.

I cannot speak too highly of the two young dead officers of mine

REPORT ON OPERATIONS 25th 26th and 27th September (Concluded)

2nd Lieutenants Basker and Hopkins. Their coolness and bravery was a great example to their men. Captain Huntington and Lieutenant Warden also rendered me good assistance and the following N C O's and men stuck it well

    C S M Biss
    Sergt Kelly
    "   Tyler
    LceCpl Robinson
    "   Kennedy
   Pte Lambley
     Carr
     Green
     Ockleford
     Davis
     Hooper
     Jeffries) Brought in wounded under heavy
     Johnson)   fire
     Feltham
  Sig.Sgt. Buckley) 8th Lincolns
  Pte   Britton)

Estree Blanche
29th September 1915

L.C. Howard Major
8th Som. L.I.

121/743

21st Division
63rd Inf Brigade.

8th Somerset L.I.
vol 2

Oct 15

WAR DIARY or INTELLIGENCE SUMMARY

Army Form C. 2118

Place	Date	Hour	Summary of Events and Information	Remarks and references to Appendices
BORRE	2-10-15		We were staying at BORRE a few days to refit and here General Forestier Walker inspected us and told us he had recommended some officers and men for honors	Appendix I
"	6-10-15		A draft of 2 + 8 N.C.O.'s and men joined us from the 3rd Battalion Somerset L.I. They were a very good lot of men and had many old soldiers among them. A	
"	9-10-15		further draft of 100 N.C.O. and men and 12 Officers joined us from the 9th Battalion Somerset L.I. The men were not do [due] for a bit as the 9th Battalion were	
"	12-10-15		They arrived without arms, rations, greatcoats ??? . We sent to STRAZEELE and while there received	
STRAZEELE	15-10-15		orders. We moved to STRAZEELE and relieving Cross by the C.W.C. We O.B. Hott was ordered there one night and stay a trench line under the	Appendix II
"	24-10-15		Then moved to LA CRECHE stayed there one night and	
ARMENTIERES	25-10-15		ARMENTIERES where we are occupying a trench line under the guidance and instruction of the 50th Division.	

L. Howard Major
Comdg 8th S.L.I
Somerset L.I.

1st November 1915

Appendix I

Schedule No. (To be left Blank).	Unit.	Regtl.No.	Rank & Name.	Action for which commended.	Recommended By.	Honour or Reward	To be left Blank.
	8 Som L.I.		Major Lewis Charles Howard.	For gallant action in holding the front line after all other troops in his vicinity had retired. Slowly withdrawing only when strong 3 German Force was within 200 yards of him.	B.C.		
	"		2nd Lt. Ian Brodie Innes.	Tending wounded under heavy fire and rallying his men.	"		
	"		Lieut. Arthur Beach Hatt.	With Sergt J. Hood and about 6 men held on to position on right of HILL 70 till about 3 p.m. after practically everyone else in the vicinity had retired.	"		
	"		Captain Richard Hall Huntington. 2nd Lt. Walter George Warden.	) Stuck to their work coolly)) and helped to hold the) (CHALK PITS.	"		
	"	12190.	Pte. Frank Arthur Jefferies.	Rescued wounded Officer			
	"	15420.	Pte. Frederick Johnson.	under heavy fire.			
	"	16100	L/Cpl John George Robinson.	) Stuck to their work with) energy and cheerfulness	"		
	"	16945	Pte. William George Feltham.	) and helped to hold the) CHALK PITS.			

"C" Form (Duplicate).   Army Form C. 2123.

MESSAGES AND SIGNALS.

INDIAN HQ
ZFC
McDrayer
9.24 AM

Service Instructions: ZFC

Appendix II

TO: SOM LI

Sender's Number	Day of Month	In reply to Number	AAA
BMX 916	Twentyfirst		

Following message received from division begins AAA The F M C in C has awarded military cross to Lieut A B HATT (8th Somerset Light Infantry) AAA Inform him and offer major generals congratulations AAA Ends.

FROM PLACE & TIME: 63rd INF BDE   9.29 PM

21st Kuraim

Ph. Somered L.I.
Vol. 3
Nov. 15

WAR DIARY of 8th (S) Batt. Somerset L.I.
INTELLIGENCE SUMMARY

Army Form C. 2118

Instructions regarding War Diaries and Intelligence Summaries are contained in F. S. Regs., Part II. and the Staff Manual respectively. Title Pages will be prepared in manuscript.

(Erase heading not required.)

Place	Date	Hour	Summary of Events and Information	Remarks and references to Appendices
ARMENTIERES	1/11/15		We continued work under the instruction of the 50th Division and from 3rd November – 10th inclusive we did trench work under the orders of the C.R.E. of that Division.	
"	8/11/15		On the 8th November a draft of 30. N.C.O's and men joined us from the Base; they were provided with iron rations and one kind of smoke helmets.	
"	10/11/15		On 10th November an enemy shell struck "C" Co's billet and caused 16 casualties among the men who were rushing into the building; of these two were killed, one seriously wounded (since died) and the remainder all slightly wounded.	
"	11/11/15		On November 11th we took over trenches 70, 71, 72 and 73 on our own; these trenches had previously been held by the 50th Division. When we took them over these trenches were in a very bad state, and as we were having a good deal of rain about this time the condition of the trenches was not improved. Our casualties were three killed and five wounded; we were relieved on the 14th by the 10th York & Lancs.	
"	14/11/15		We were in rest billets for three days during which time we furnished working parties for the R.E.'s and we returned to the trenches on November 17th.	

Army Form C. 2118

WAR DIARY
or
INTELLIGENCE SUMMARY
(Erase heading not required.)

Instructions regarding War Diaries and Intelligence Summaries are contained in F. S. Regs., Part II. and the Staff Manual respectively. Title Pages will be prepared in manuscript.

Place	Date	Hour	Summary of Events and Information	Remarks and references to Appendices
ARMENTIERES	17/11/15		On Nov 19th 2nd Lieut Sutts was severely wounded in the leg and hand while out on a daring reconnaissance with 2nd Lieut Morgan and L.Corp Jennings. The two officers were recommended for the Military Cross and L.Corp Jennings was promoted Corporal.	app - 1.
	19/11/15			
	20/11/15		On December 20th 2nd Lt Parramor went to Hospital and he has not rejoined as yet	app - 2
	21/11/15		We were relieved on the 21st by the 10th York & Lancs. and went back to our usual billets for four days.	
	25/11/15		We provided working parties on the 23rd and 24th (about 500 men each time) and were inspected by G.O.C. Division on the morning of the 25th, before returning to the trenches in the evening.	
	29/11/15		We were in the trenches from the 25th - 29th and during that time we had four casualties - two killed and two wounded, one of whom has since died. We are now back in billets for four days.	

Howard [signature]
Major [signature]

Schedule No. (To be left Blank).	UNIT.	Regtl. No.	Rank and Name.	Action for which commended.	Recommended By.	Honour or Reward	(To be left Blank).
	9th (S) Battn Somerset L.I.		2nd Lieut Jukes. Cecil Burnell. 2nd Lieut Morgan. Alfred Paul.	During reconnaissance on night of 19th November 1915. These two officers and one private went to enemy's wire to locate snipers post and m.g. emplacement, with intention of bombing them. While at the enemy's barbed wire m.g. opened fire on them before they had time to throw their bombs, seriously wounding 2nd Lieut Jukes who was carried back to our own lines by 2nd Lieut Morgan	[signature] Lt Col Comdg 9th S.H.L.I. [signature]	Military Cross	

63rd Brigade. 21st Division. 2nd Corps.

Corps Register No.

appx 1

App. 2.

WAR DIARY
or
INTELLIGENCE SUMMARY

Army Form C. 2118

Place	Date	Hour	Summary of Events and Information	Remarks and references to Appendices
			Extract from Batt. Orders 21st November 1915.	
			Para. 44. Promotion. The Commanding Officer has been pleased to approve of the following promotion:—	
			No 18926. L/Cpl Jennings. A. "C" Co. to be Actg. Cpl. for gallantry in the field.	
			Certified true copy.	
			R.S.W. Huskands	
			2nd Lt. ag. adjt 1/12/15	

8th Som: L.I.
Vol: 4
November 1915

121/7931

42

Minor enterprise 15/16th Dec.
Death of Lt Col Howard

WAR DIARY
INTELLIGENCE SUMMARY

Sheet 1.

Army Form C. 2118

Place: ARMENTIERES.

8th Bn. Somerset L.I.

Date	Hour	Summary of Events and Information	Remarks and references to Appendices
Dec. 1st, 2nd		At beginning of the month we were in billets. A draft of 32 N.C.O.'s and men arrived late at night from the Base on the 2nd, but they were provided with iron ration and one gas helmet.	
3rd		The following morning, another draft of 40 N.C.O.'s and men joined us from the 2nd Entrenching Bn. They had 2 more helmets and iron ration. That evening we went back to the trenches for a period of 6 days.	
6th		2/Lt Barker joined the Bn. on 6th and was posted to "B" Coy. We had a lot of rain while we were in the trenches this time, and the water was knee deep in most places.	
9th		We were relieved on the night of 9–10th by the 16th York Lancs and returned to our usual rest billets in the town. On this occasion we were out of the trenches for eight days during which time arrangements were made and practices carried out for a "Cutting out" enterprise on the German front line trenches. Appendix I contains the operation orders for the occasion. The men and officers for this went all volunteers.	Appx. I.
16th		The attack was made from the MUSHROOM early on the morning of the 16th Dec.; the York & Lancs and the Rodding the trenches and on their right were the 4th Middlesex. Everything went smoothly and the attack was carried out precisely as ordered. The enterprise was very successful and our men returned to our trenches without a single casualty. We captured seven Germans (four of whom were wounded) including one acting Serjeant Major, documents, papers & letters and various trench stores such as bombs &c. after the return to the MUSHROOM the German artillery woke up and they shelled our trenches very heavily for about an hour and a half.	

WAR DIARY

INTELLIGENCE SUMMARY — Sheet 2.

Place: ARMENTIERES.

Date	Hour	Summary of Events and Information	Remarks and references to Appendices
Dec br. 16th		During this bombardment we sustained seven casualties – 3 killed and 4 wounded. After the bombardment the attacking party returned to billets, and had a days sleep. The following morning the attacking party was inspected by the Corps Commander who was attended by G.O.C's Division and Brigade. The Corps Commander warmly congratulated the officers, NCO's and men on the success of the enterprise. In connection with the attack Capt Thursby tin (O.C. Party) was recommended for the D.S.O., 2nd Lt Withers (first to enter German trenches) for the Military Cross, and Sgt. Green (who was missed by 3 Germans, two of whom he afterwards killed and the third captured) APP II. Capt Fenwick and Pte Jeffries for the D.C.M. Also was recommendations were on the immediate list, while on the waiting list 2nd Lt Wright (Military Cross) and Sgt Black (D.C.M.) We returned to our trenches on the evening of the 17th.	APP II. APP III.
17th 18th To 21st		A lively time in the trenches. The enemy making several attempts to take the mine sap. Sgt Black and Pte Jeffries both distinguished themselves on the night of the 20th. Sgt Black, grenadier, when very seriously wounded continued to give directions until carried away, and Pte Jeffries, a bomber, protecting a working party in the mine crater, drove off German patrol. He was killed before he could return. Both recommended for D.C.M. Returned to Billets. In Billets.	
21st to night 24th. 24th To 28th. night		night 24th returned to trenches till night 28th. Heavy bombardment of enemy trenches front line, to which fairly heavy damage was done. Enemy replied doing damage to support trenches Yorkshire. Casualties 2 killed 2 wounded. Returned from 9th Bn.	

Army Form C. 2118

WAR DIARY

INTELLIGENCE SUMMARY

(Erase heading not required.)

3rd Sheet.

Instructions regarding War Diaries and Intelligence Summaries are contained in F. S. Regs., Part II. and the Staff Manual respectively. Title Pages will be prepared in manuscript.

Place	Date	Hour	Summary of Events and Information	Remarks and references to Appendices
ARMENTIERES	Dec. Nights 23 & 24.		On the nights 23-24th II Coy relieved a company of 10 Somersets in the MUSHROOM, Lt Colonel Howard accompanying them. Lt. Col. Howard when reconnoitering between the craters was unfortunately shot, his body was brought in that night and was buried in the afternoon of the 24th. The Corps, Division, and Brigade Commanders being present. Notification of the award of the D.S.O. for gallant work on the nights 15-16 December and on 25 & 26 September 1915 was received but too late to acquaint him before he proceeded to the trenches.	

A.W. Phillipps
Commanding
31.12.1915. 8th Somerset L.I. 9.

SECRET.

App I

BATTALION OPERATION ORDERS NO.13 by LT.COL.L.C.HOWARD
COMMANDING 8th (S) BATTALION SOMERSET LIGHT INFANTRY.

Reference Sheet 36   1/10000.   Field.
                                                      14th December 1915

1. Intention.

An attack will be made on the enemy's position East of ARMENTIERES on the morning of the 16th December, 1915 for the purpose of:-
(a) Gaining information from prisoners.
(b) Destroying enemy's trenches.
(c) Discovering how his trenches are held.
(d) Causing casualties among his supports and reserves by making them become vulnerable targets for our Artillery.
(e) Further decreasing his morale.
(f) Destroying Mine Shaft, if found.

2. Objective.

The objective will be the enemy's two Lines of trenches and dug-outs, penetrating as far as Stream which runs parallel in rear of the 2nd German Trench, and extending laterally from I 11 c 6.6½ to I 11 c 5.2½

3. Attacking Troops.

The attacking party will be under the Command of Captain Huntington and will consist of 6 Officers and 117 N.C.Os. and men, distributed as follows:-
  5 Scouts (with wire cutters) under C.S.M. Smith.
  4 Wire Cutters   :   2nd Lt. Withers.
  16 Roller Mat Men.   :   :   :   :
  4 Bridging Ladder Men   :   :   :   :
  5 Squads of Bombers under 2nd Lt. Wright and Vernon.
  R.E. Party with explosives.
  16 Bayonet Men under 2nd Lt. Morgan, to search dug-outs and kill all Germans offering resistance.
  10 Men under Lt. Hatt to keep up communication and to take charge of all prisoners. The scouts will also assist Lt. Hatt in this.
  4 men who will carry steps and who will act as orderlies and stay with O.C. attacking party.
  3 Signallers to establish communication with Bay 13 Trench 70.

The wire cutters, roller mat men, and bridging ladder men under 2nd Lt. Withers on arrival at the enemy's trenches will proceed to search all dug-outs to left of breach, following 2nd Lt. Wright and his bombers. They will bayonet all enemy offering resistance. 16 Bayonet men under 2nd Lt. Morgan will follow 2nd Lt. Vernon and his bombers to right of breach, searching all dug-outs.

The wire cutters should pay attention to all barbed wire only, and should not attempt to cut smooth wire. All men must be prepared to hear the enemy speak in English, and must not be taken unawares by this ruse. All men who have white faces must be bayoneted. All wires in enemy's trenches must be cut.

4. Bombing Squads.

The Bombing Squads will be made up as follows:-
No.1 Squad, which will work to left of breach under 2nd Lt. Wright.
  4 Bayonet Men.
  4 Throwers.
  4 Carriers, (each with apron and Nose Bag of Bombs).
  4 Wire Men also carrying 25 bombs each in Nose Bag.

4. Bombing Squads (Contd).

2 Bayonet men, one with shovel, and one with pick slung across back by rifle sling.

No.2 Squad which will work to right of breach under 2nd Lt.Vernon will be composed similarly to No.1 Squad. These squads Nos.1 and 2 will work outwards along both trenches for 100 yards until communication trench is reached, when they will block both trenches and hold until signal for withdrawal.

No.3 squad under Sergeant Black, composed as under, will follow No.1 squad to left, but will block communication trench at Stream on arrival there. This will be held until signal for withdrawal.

    2 Bayonet men.
    2 Carriers.
    1 Wire man also carrying 25 bombs in Nose Bag.
    1 Bayonet man with pick and shovel slung across back.

No.4 squad under Corporal Fenwick will follow No.2 squad to right, and will block and hold communication trench at stream until withdrawal signal. It will be composed similarly to No.3 Squad.

No.5 squad under L/Corporal Hullah, will proceed up SEARCHLIGHT AVENUE as far as stream, and will block and hold 2 minutes after withdrawal signal. This squad will be composed similarly to No.3.

No.3, 4 and 5 Squads will destroy bridges over stream.

5. Equipment.

All Officers and men will blacken faces and hands. This together with a counter-sign, will serve as a means of recognition, besides helping to hide the attacking troops, and also upsetting morale of enemy. Each man to go as lightly as possible. No haversacks, packs, gum boots or water bottles to be carried. No caps will be worn, but Gas Helmets will be worn, rolled up to fit round forehead. All possible means of identification, such as mark on clothing, badges, etc, or any article which might give a clue to enemy will be removed from men. All bayonets will be darkened. All watches to be carefully compared at 9 a.m. and again at 9 p.m. on the 15th. Gloves will be worn by wire cutters. Every man of the attacking party will be instructed in the use of a Mills Grenade, and will carry one in each side pocket. Every Group Commander will carry a flashlight. All Officers and N.C.Os. to carry whistles. All Officers to carry Very Pistols with red and blue lights.

Lt.Hatts Party will be equipped as follows:-
5 men with picks and 5 with shovels slung across their backs by rifle slings, and 5 of them will carry Nose Bags with bombs, which they will deposit with C.O. at I 11 c 5.6
The 4 C.O's orderlies will also carry picks and shovels slung across their backs.

6. Patrol.

An Officers patrol under 2nd Lt. Wallis will leave Bay 13 Trench 70 at 10.30 p.m. and will report on wire cutting etc.

7. Assault.

5 Scouts under C.S.M.Smith will leave at 2.45 a.m. to find best gaps in wire and guide assaulting party through All other men will be assembled behind Bays 12,13 and 14, Trench 70, by 2.50 a.m. At 3 a.m. they will begin crawling noiselessly out, and will make their way as noiselessly as possible towards assaulting points I 11 c 5.5

BATTALION OPERATION ORDERS NO.13 (Contd).

7. Assault. (contd).

which they will reach at 3.15 a.m. 12 men of supports will remove our knife rests in order that assaulting party may pass through. The wire cutters will leave followed by the mat and Bridging Ladder Carriers under 2nd Lt.Withers. These will be followed immediately by the 5 Bombing Squads in succession, the R.E. Party going with No.2 Bombing Squad. The Bayonet Men under 2nd Lt.Morgand will then follow, and lastly will come Lt.Hatts Squad, signallers, and O.C. Attacking Party. Should there be any delay at enemy's wire, should enemy open fire, bombers will kneel down and bomb front line trenches into quiescence whilst obstacles are being overcome, upon which the bombers will lead into enemy's trenches followed by 2nd Lt.Withers squad, followed again by 2nd Lt.Morgan with R.E. Party, followed in turn by Lieut. Hatts squad. If quick release block is anywhere met with, it must be rushed by bayonet without any hesitation.

8. Withdrawal.

The signal for withdrawal will be the "rally" blown on whistle and a succession of red and blue very lights and will be given not later than 3.35 a.m. Both signals will be used and should be repeated by all Officers, but either signal will be authority for withdrawal. Lieut.Hatt and prisoners with escort will be first to withdraw followed by 2nd Lt.Morgan, who will line parapet with his 16 men until all are clear. He will retain the position until ordered to retire by O.C. 2nd Lt.Withers party will follow 2nd Lt. Morgans out of the trenches, and they will be followed by bombing squads in the following order:- 1,3,4,5 and 2. The R.E. party will leave the No.2 bombing squad.

9. Artillery Preparation.

In addition to other gaps, a gap of 50 yards will be made during the 15th December from I 11 c 6.5 to I 11 c 5.4. At 3.18 a.m., artillery will open fire on both flanks, and also on support trenches, thus giving protection against counter-attack. They will also bombard points in rear where enemy supports and reserves are likely to be on the move for counter-attack.

Trench Mortars.

Trench Mortars will commence at 3.18 a.m. and will heavily bombard enemy's support trenches, and also front line trenches on either flank, paying particular attention to Machine Gun Emplacements.

Rifle Grenades.

Rifle Grenades will be fired into enemy's front line trenches on either flank, commencing at 3.18 a.m.

Machine Guns.

12 guns will be used. 8 guns will be placed on our parapet and will sweep enemy's parapet, beginning at 3.18 a.m. from I 11 c 4.0 to I 18 d 2.6 and from I 11 c 6.8 to I 11 a 6.8
4 Guns will remain in Concrete Emplacement.
The Machine Gun at PORT EGAL REDOUBT will also open fire on selected targets in rear of enemy's trenches.

BATTALION OPERATION ORDERS NO.13 (CONTD).

9. Artillery Preparation Continued.

<u>Rifle Batteries and Snipers</u>, will fire with increased activity all day, and will open fire on selected targets at 3.18 a.m.

<u>Rifle Fire</u>, on selected targets in rear to be kept up slowly each night, so that firing on night of 15th, to hide any noise our concentrations may make, will not make enemy suspicious.

Very Lights to be used very sparingly, and only when necessary, so that the absence of them during our concentration will not arouse enemy.

10. Supports.

A party of ten men with eight stretcher bearers under 2nd Lt. Akerman will take up position 50 yards in front of enemy trenches. They will remain in position until the whole of the assaulting party pass through them on return journey.

A party of twenty men will remain in supports with O.C. Battalion behind Bays 12, 13 and 14 to reinforce if called upon by assaulting officer to do so.

11. Positions.

Position of O.C. Assaulting Party will be at centre of breach in enemy's trenches I 11 c 5.4½.

Position of O.C. Battalion will be Bay 13, Trench 70 where telephonic communication with O.C. Attacking Party will be established immediately after assault.

12. Aid Posts.

Aid Posts will be established at FIVE DUG OUTS.

(sgd) L.C. Howard. Lt.Col.
Commanding 8th Bn. Somerset L.I.

Report by Lieut. Shepherd R.E. In Charge of
Party which tried to discover Mine
Shaft on Night 15th/16.

I reached the German Parapet accompanied by Corporal Cooke and Sapper Oliver with the charge (which consisted of 49 lb of Guncotton) at 3.15 a.m. in accordance with pre-arranged scheme.

I bored down to the South following along the Fire Trench and examining all dug-outs and any other likely places for a Mine Shaft. The only thing I saw of any special interest was what I took to be an electric pump in a flooded dug-out. I also noticed two cables a little thicker than the ordinary signalling cable running al along the interior slope of parapet of Fire Trench held on white porcelain bobbins. I looked particularly carefully for a shaft near the sire where we had suspected one to be from observation from our own trenches, but could see no signs of one.

At 3.25 a.m. I had reached the extreme Southern limit of the portion of trench occupied by our troops. Here I discovered an octogonal Steel Machine Gun Emplacement placed some way out in the thick parapet of Fire Trench to which access was gained by a narrow passage way. The Machine Gun appeared to be on top and I think was of a disappearing type but I cannot be certain on this point.

I got two of the Infantry to cover me a little further down the trench and placed the charge on the floor of the Emplacement having lighted the fuse. The charge exploded as I retired.

(sgd) N.Shepherd. Lt.
171 Tunnelling Company R.E.

Report on the Action of the Machine Guns during the
Minor Enterprise carried out on Night 15th/16th.

Eleven Machine Guns of the Brigade took part in the Enterprise, and were supported by 2 Sections of the 4th Motor Machine Gun Battery.

Disposition of Machine Guns.

Eight machine guns, four on either side of the MUSHROOM, were placed in position at dusk with instructions to sweep enemy parapet from I 11 c 4.1 to I 16 d 2.6 and from I 11 c 6.8 to I 11 a 5.5 till our men had returned to our trenches and to silence any hostile machine guns that opened fire. When our men had returned four of these eight guns were placed again in their concrete emplacements, the other four remaining on the parapet and continuing to sweep enemy parapet at intervals.

One gun was placed in the MUSHROOM with instructions not to fire unless the enemy counter-attacked.

Two guns searched by indirect fire PREMESQUES Road and SEARCHLIGHT STREET and swept the WEZ MACQUART - ARRET Road from I 17 b 3.1 to I 17 b 7.5. These guns were laid by day and fired from positions near PORT EGAL REDOUBT. Two sections (4 guns) of the 4th Motor Machine Gun Battery searched the LILLE ROAD, WEZ MACQUART and Communication Trenches on either side of the village from positions near LILLE POST. 20,000 rounds were expended during the night by the Machine Guns.

Report on German Wire opposite the Mushroom.

The German wire is three knife rests thick. The outer rows are straight and the middle row is zig-zag as shown.

2. The knife rests are about the same size as ours and are not dug in. They are all made of smooth wire stretched across between the ends, bound in between with heavy coils of thick barbed wire. There are no knife rests with more than six coils, and some have only four. All the knife rests were joined together by smooth wire.

There were no signs of recent work on the wire, and the smooth wire in some places is badly in need of repair.
The coils of barbed wire are fastened to the plain wire by very thin wire like string, which is old and very rotten, and is easily pulled off.

These coils of barbed wire are very thick and difficult to cut with the 10" wire cutters issued to Infantry: the 14" wire cutters supplied to the Royal Engineers are admirably suited to cutting this wire.

G535/4

S E C R E T.

REPORT ON A MINOR ENTERPRISE

carried out by the

8th SOMERSET L.I., 63rd INFANTRY BRIGADE, 21st DIVISION

on the night of the 15th/16th December 1915.

****

1. Objects of Operation.

The enterprise was a "cutting out" expedition with the following objects:-
(a) To kill as many Germans as possible.
(b) To take some prisoners for identification.
(c) To destroy a mine shaft, if found.
(d) To ascertain whether arrangements for installing gas had been made.

2. Strength of Force.

Previous reconnaissances had shown that the enemy's sentries are not always on the alert.
It was realised that this might mean that the front trenches were only lightly held, in which case a small force would have sufficed. However, it was decided that the importance of maintaining the fighting spirit of the men was paramount and to make the strength of the attacking party as large as possible in consonance with the objects to be attained. The strength was limited to 120 men, who were selected from volunteers.

3. Selection of Objective.

It had been previously decided that the attack should be made from Trench 70 (The MUSHROOM). In order to justify the successful employment of as large a force as contemplated in para. 2, it was essential that :-
(a) The attack should be a surprise.
(b) The distance to be traversed should be as short as possible.
(c) The portion of the enemy's line to be attacked should, if possible, include a main communication trench as this would probably ensure that the trench at this point was held, and officers' dugouts and machine gun emplacements might reasonably be expected to be found near this point.
Accordingly the portion of the enemy's line selected to be attacked was from I.11.c.5.2½ to I.11.c.6.6½ which included the main communication trench (SEARCHLIGHT STREET) at I.11.c.5.4½.
The disadvantages of this objective were :-
(a) The advance was completely enfiladed from the Railway Salient I.11.a.3.2.
(b) No covered lines of approach were available.

4. Preliminary Training and Preparations.

The men selected for the enterprise were billeted together. Trenches were dug according to scale to represent the German trenches from I.11.c.6.6½ to I.11.c.5.2½ as taken from an aeroplane photograph. The attack was practised by day and

and by night for three days, each man using the exact tools he would use in the actual attack. Consequently each man knew his place thoroughly, and the attack went like clockwork. The men practised the attack for the last time at 5 a.m. on the morning of the 15th. They then rested all day.

5. Preliminary Reconnaissances.

Previous Reconnaissances were carried out very thoroughly by Officers, and the presence of a ditch believed to exist between the enemy's wire and parapet was confirmed. Some chunks were cut out of the enemy's wire on night of 13th. The enemy's listening post was invariably found unoccupied.

6. Artillery Preparation.

A preliminary artillery bombardment took place on December 8th, and on December 15th a very complete bombardment was carried out for the purpose of cutting the enemy's wire in three places and destroying his machine gun emplacements and parapets. The wire opposite the point of attack was well cut in places sufficient to allow the Infantry to pass through. As a measure of precaution mats were taken and these proved very useful to throw across the loose wire.

The O.C., 8th Somerset L.I., spent the day with the F.O.O. and watched the bombardment of the enemy's machine gun emplacements and the wire cutting, taking note of the exact bearing of the best path made through the enemy's wire.

7. Attacking Troops.

The attacking party under the command of Captain Huntington, consisted of 6 Officers and 117 N.C.Os. and men, distributed as follows:-
- 5 Scouts (with wire cutters) under C.S.M. Smith.
- 4 wire cutters, 16 roller mat men, 4 bridging ladder men under 2nd Lieut. Withers.
- 5 squads of grenadiers under 2nd Lieuts. Wright and Vernon.
- R.E. party under Lieut. Shepherd.
- 18 bayonet men under 2nd Lieut Morgan.
- 10 men under Lieut. Hatt to keep up communication and to take charge of all prisoners.
- 4 men to carry steps and act as orderlies for O.C. attacking party.
- 3 signallers to establish communication with British trenches.

8. Narrative of Events, December 16th.

(a) Preliminary Reconnaissance. At 12.15 a.m. 16th December a patrol was sent out under 2nd Lieut Wallis to find out if enemy's listening post was occupied, and to see if enemy were on the alert.

The patrol spent twenty minutes at enemy's wire, and were not fired at. They returned at 1.30 a.m. and reported listening post unoccupied, enemy not alert and sounds of whistling and talking coming from their trench.

(b) The advance. At 2.45 a.m. the concentration being complete, the order was given for the bridging ladders and mats to be taken over the parapet. This was done, and the men followed them, and lay down behind our knife rests in the correct order for the advance. At 3 a.m. the knife rests were noiselessly removed, and the signal given for the advance, which was carried out very quietly and slowly.

Page 3.

The officer leading the advance took with him a roll of broad white ribbon, one end of which was left in Bay 13, and moving on a bearing of 118 degrees magnetic, unrolled the ribbon as he went, leaving behind a white path from our trenches to the point in the German wire where a path had been cut. He passed the ribbon through the German wire and tied it beyond the wire. This ribbon was most effective as it ensured the men finding the best way through the enemy's wire, and also the right way home again.

(c) Passage & Obstacles. 2nd Lieut. Wither's Party was the first to reach the enemy's wire. The men put down their mats over the broken knife rests, and the whole assaulting party then crossed the wire and ditch by the mats, without the slightest noise.

(d) Entry into German Trench. They then extended along the German parapet and crawled up to the top of it, from whence 2nd Lieut. Withers saw three men talking together in the trench. He shot one and jumped into the trench closely followed by the whole party. The other two men tried to run and were bayonetted. 2nd Lieut Withers entered the German trench at about 3.18 a.m. and the last man got in about 3.20 a.m. just as the guns commenced.

(e) The artillery barrage was provided by two field batteries, some heavy guns and trench mortars on the rear and flanks of the trench to be entered. In addition three squads of rifle grenadiers fired on the enemy's trenches on each flank of that attacked.

(f) The enemy was completely surprised and the assaulting troops were into the trenches before any alarm was given, notwithstanding the fact that a few Very lights were sent up close on the flanks, during the advance across NO MAN'S LAND. The men were very steady, however, and remained motionless whenever a light was up.

(g) A few of the enemy showed fight. Three men tried to rush Sergeant Coxon, but he shot two with his revolver and took the third man prisoner. The officer would not surrender and had to be shot.

(h) Lieutenant Shepherd, R.E., searched for the mine shaft but could not find it, and so exploded his charge in a steel machine gun emplacement.

(j) One machine gun, which was not even loaded, was taken out of the trench, but the men could not unfix it from its stand, and it was abandoned in the German ditch, as it was extremely heavy, the mud was very deep, and the sides of the ditch very steep and slippery. All removable articles were taken away, all telephone wires cut, and some bombs were exploded in each dug-out on leaving them. There were no gas cylinders in the trench.

(k) Withdrawal. At 3.35 a.m. the signal for retirement was given, and the return to our trenches was all completed by 3.50 a.m. The whole enterprise was carried out without a single casualty. Later, after returning to our trenches, the attacking force lost 3 killed and 7 wounded from hostile shell fire. Seven prisoners were captured and twenty men killed. The remainder fled.

9. Strength of Enemy.

The enemy's trenches are not strongly held. The attack embraced a front of about 150 yards of their trench, but only twenty of the enemy were killed, and about the same number fled along the flanks and communication trenches in front of our bombers, and were undoubtedly caught by our shell fire there. This, with the seven prisoners we took,

Page 4.

would appear to be all the men that were occupying 150 yards of front line trench.

10. Communications.

Communication was quickly established between the German trench and Trench 70, but communication to Brigade Headquarters failed. Nine orderlies in all were employed, but all were either killed or wounded. Practically from the beginning all the wires were cut except one artillery wire.

COMMENTS.

1. The success of the operation was due to careful preparation, the good discipline of the troops and the assistance of the artillery, both in the preliminary bombardment and in the accurate and well timed barrage during the attack.

2. The time selected for the attack was purposely fixed for an hour and a half after the moon had set, as it was thought that if the attack did not take place soon after the moon had set, the enemy might relax their vigilance. In point of actual fact, this apparently did happen. The night was very dark and wet and admirably suited to an enterprise of this nature.

3. The plan of blackening faces and wearing smoke helmets undoubtedly proved of great help in distinguishing between friend and foe.

4. The white ribbon tape proved most useful in marking the route both to and from the enemy's trench.

5. There appeared to be no sentries keeping a proper lookout, or our advance must have been detected.

6. The machine gun detachments were either absent from their posts or had bolted, for no fire from machine guns molested our advance or worried our withdrawal. The captured gun had its cover on!

7. The German officers and their men appear to have discarded or were not wearing their equipment, and had no rifles or other weapons handy to repel an attack; for they made no resistance with their fire-arms, which might ordinarily have been expected.

8. Although provided with elaborate anti-gas masks, they were not on the person but found lying about.

9. Discipline appeared to be very slack, especially with the officers - e.g. taking off their equipment and leaving it in their dug-outs.

10. Notwithstanding our bombardment having cut their wire, they made no attempts to watch the gaps and cover them by rifle or machine gun fire. It should naturally have appeared to them that the fact of our artillery firing so persistently at their obstacles foreshadowed some further designs on them.

11. There seemed to be no arrangements to counter-attack and retake lost trenches, since no attempt was made in the 20 minutes the trenches were occupied.

****

2nd Army.

G.13.

Below is a drawing of a mat used by 21st Division for crossing barbed wire entanglements

It is found best to roll up the mat from both ends, so that when it is thrown over the wire a sufficient length hangs down on both sides of it.

Mat for crossing wire.

slats
3' x 1½" x ½"
(gabion pickets)
1½" apart.

Canvas nailed to Slats in four places.

12'.0"

3'.0"

Method of using.-

Carried rolled.

When required to be used two men (facing each other) get hold of the roll, one at each end, and swing it out in the required direction holding on to the two corners (of one end). The mat unrolls itself easily. Unrolling should be practised. Slats should be uppermost when mat is unrolled.

SECRET.

Notes on Operation of December 15th/16th, 1915.

21st Divisional Artillery.

21st Division.

1. The attached copy of orders issued shews full details of tasks and ammunition allotted. These were carried out as arranged and no difficulty was experienced.
   The procedure produced no new lessons, but again emphasised :-
   (a) that 18-pr shrapnel may be a very effective wire-cutting projectile, both when burst on percussion and in air, at ranges of 2,500 to 3,000 yards.
   (b) that 4.5" H.E. is not so effective against wire.
   (c) that 4.5" Howitzers can be used with tremendous effect on the front line of trenches. The damage done to the parapets by 4.5" shell is very great.

2. During the fire an excessive amount of smoke was noticed from all guns. White puffs of smoke continued to be emitted even after the guns had been firing for some considerable time.
   During the night - the official time as recognised by G.O.C. 63rd Infantry Brigade was sent to all R.A. Units at 3.10 a.m., the result being that all guns opened fire at exact moment.
   Again there was no hitch in the arrangements, The guns employed against the line North of the Railway Salient were stopped when it was presumed that the Infantry had returned, the remainder kept up the barrage and bombardment until the report that all were back was received.
   Difficulty of Communications - the excessive noise prevented messages being sent through on the D.3 telephone.

3. The details of wire-cutting may be of interest.
   Batteries were detailed to cut wire at the following places :-
   I.11.c.6.5., I.5.c.7.1. and I.17.a.2.8. The result being reported as satisfactory in all cases.
   The Officer Commanding the assaulting party remained with the Forward Observing Officer directing the fire against I.11.c.6.5., so that the fire could be continued until he was satisfied that the obstacle had been removed.
   The place where the wire was most efficiently cut was noted by the Infantry Commander and no difficulty was experienced in finding the path when the moment of assault came.
   Two 18-pr. batteries and one howitzer battery were detailed to cut the wire from I.11.c.6.5. to a point 50 yards to the South.
   The Southernmost portion was cut most effectively and it is reported that the damage done was entirely due to the fire of one 18-pr. battery. The 4.5" howitzer shell did little damage to the wire but was extremely effective on the parapets.

The following....

2.

The following are the details of the shooting of the
18-pr. battery ("A"/96) mentioned above :-

TARGET:- Three rows of knife rests with very thick wire on
a front of 25 yards. Target on the same level as gun
and the ground between trenches was flat and level.

4 guns fired from very good platforms made of
sleepers with 3" planks nailed on top. The guns
were not anchored but wheels were scotched with
sandbags and the trail butted against a baulk. All
platforms were similar. The range was 2,650 yards.
300 rounds shrapnel, fuze 80 were used.
Two lanes, one 12 yards wide and the other 5 yards
wide were cut. The lanes were absolutely free of
wire and the wire on the remaining part of the front
allotted was considerably damaged.

A selection from 1,000 rounds of ammunition was made,
so that the variation due to different lots should
be the minimum. As it was, about 70 different lots,
bearing consecutive numbers, were used, but care was
taken that the ammunition was expended in sequence of
lots. Battery fire was the method of fire employed
and the rate varied from 10 seconds to 2 seconds.
The fire was controlled by the F.O.O. in the trench and
great skill was shown by this officer. A fuze length
was ordered at the start and neither it or the corrector
was altered throughout. A large percentage burst
on percussion and it is reported that the effect from
such bursts was greater than from those bursting
low in air. It was found that the guns did not remain
absolutely steady and that relaying was necessary
(especially with sight clinometer) after each round.

The second 18-pr. battery ("B"/96) also fired
300 rounds shrapnel at the northern half of the
allotted front. Here the wire was not so thoroughly
cut, but lanes were cut through it.

4. Counter-Battery work.

Counter-Battery work was arranged for by day and night.
One 60-pr and one 4.5" howitzer battery being kept in the
hands of the Divisional Artillery Commander for the purpose.
These engaged hostile batteries by day.
When the enemy opened fire on our trenches after
the attack, a large number of flashes were seen. Numerous
batteries have been located by the flash-spotting stations,
but on account of lack of information as to which were active
at the time, the counter-batteries were not employed by
night.

5. Telephone Communication.

During the bombardment and wire cutting by day, Forward
Observing officers from the Batteries engaged were up in
the Front Trenches. Communications worked very well and there
was no difficulty.

At night, when our attack took place, a Forward
Officer from one of the Batteries accompanied the O.C. Battalion
making the attack. He remained in our Front trench with the
Battalion Commander during the whole time. Communications worked
well until our batteries opened fire for the barrage, and the
enemy guns replied on to our front trenches. The noise was then
so great that difficulty was experienced in sending messages
back, also wires which had been laid down our communication
trenches were cut. One D.5 buried line remained intact
throughout.

If the operation....

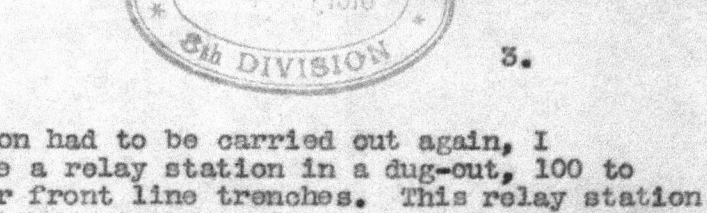

3.

If the operation had to be carried out again, I would certainly have a relay station in a dug-out, 100 to 200 yards behind our front line trenches. This relay station would be provided with an instrument tapped in, an operator and two linemen. This would, I am convinced, be of great advantage.

6. **Co-operation between Infantry and Artillery.**

The plans for the operation were arranged by the infantry and artillery together, and there was therefore no hitch at all in carrying out the orders.

During the bombardment and wire-cutting by day, the Officer Commanding the battalion which was going to make the attack was actually with the Forward Observing Officers of the heavy batteries and 18-pr. batteries, which were engaged on the most important points. He was therefore able to see for himself that the artillery work was being done as he wished.

During the attack by night, there was a Forward Officer with the Battalion Commander, and a Liaison Officer with the O.C. Infantry Brigade.

To this close co-operation between the infantry and Artillery, both before and during the operations, a large measure of the success must be attributed.

(sgd) R. WELLESLEY,
Brig.-General,
Commanding 21st Divisional Arty.

H.Q. 21st Div. Arty.
18th December, 1915.

SECRET.

Account of an enterprise carried out on Second Army front
on night of December 15th/16th.
========== * ==========

1.   An enterprise was carried out by the 8th Somerset Light Infantry, 21st Division, last night, the 15th/16th, with the object of searching for mineshafts and destroying them if found, as well as to capture prisoners, inflict loss on the enemy and lower his moral.

2.   During the 15th a bombardment of the enemy's trenches was carried out by the Divisional and Heavy Artillery. The wire was cut by Field Artillery in 4 or 5 places and salients, strong points and machine gun positions from which fire was likely to be brought to bear on the attack were damaged by howitzers. The wire at the point of assault was found to be sufficiently destroyed, and there was no difficulty in getting into the trenches, but some at least of the attacking troops crossed the wire by means of mats.   That the fire of the howitzers was effective is shown by the fact that the infantry were subjected to no rifle or machine gun fire during the operation. The assaulting troops consisted of 5 Officers and 130 men of the 8th Somerset Light Infantry who advanced from the trench known as the MUSHROOM in I.11.d, Sheet 36, at 3-15 a.m. and rushed over the enemy's wire and into the trench without a pause. At 3-18, just as the infantry reached the enemy's wire our Artillery opened fire on the German front trenches on the flanks of the attack and on the communication and support trenches in rear of the part to be assaulted. This artillery fire was supplemented by trench mortar fire and rifle grenades on the flanks of the portion to be assaulted. The fire was very accurate and to the correct timing and accuracy of this fire the infantry ascribe the success of the operations.

3.

3.   The men had their faces blackened, which apparently frightened the Saxons, and such as were not shot or bayoneted at the first rush ran down the communication trenches. Grenades were taken by our men but were little used, most of the work being done with the bayonet. The majority of the garrison appear to have been in their deep dug-outs and were all put out of action. Seven prisoners were brought back, of whom four were unwounded. 48 German dead are stated to have been counted in the trench, and it is thought that our artillery and machine gun fire on the trenches in rear inflicted numerous additional casualties. There was practically no opposition and the attack was a complete surprise. At the end of 20 minutes the infantry were withdrawn. The attacking force had no casualties either in the advance or retirement but two men were hit in our own trenches after getting back.

4.   The German retaliation on our front trenches was accurate and severe but was not put into operation for some 20 minutes after the assault. Some 30 casualties resulted from this retaliation.

5.   The German front trenches are reported to have been dry and clean but the back trenches were wet. No mineshafts could be found and there were no gas installations. A steel and concrete machine gun emplacement was blown up. The gun was brought away but it was very heavy and could not be got back to our trench. It was therefore thrown into a deep ditch in front of the enemy's parapet from which it is hoped to recover it later. Gas masks, oxygen apparatus, grenades, Very's pistol lights and other trophies were brought back to our lines.

SECRET.

99C/GS/328.
27/12-15

Account of a Minor Operation carried out by
2nd Canadian Division on 15th December.
-------- * --------

After artillery preparation extending over several periods in cutting wire and shelling various trenches in rear, a "cutting out" enterprise was carried out at 4 a.m. 15th December on the enemy's advanced barrier on the MESSINES - PLOEGSTEERT road at U.8 c.9.9. This had been in process of improvement and consolidation by the enemy for a fortnight past although knocked about from time to time recently by our artillery. A sap had been run out from our trench on the west side of the road, our men working the past three nights and a sap-head had been made within bombing distance of the barrier (about 25 yards).

The attack was made in two parties, one on each side of road, and went in after the barricade had been bombarded by a field gun in position at our front line barricade. Of the enemy's garrison of 6 men four were killed and the other two brought out as prisoners, unwounded. A varied lot of equipment and personal effects was secured including several rifles (one a Ross) and a number of hand grenades (two British Mills) there was also a pioneer's saw-edged bayonet. There were no respirators.

The attack of the barrier following immediately on the gun fire was done with bombs and the bayonet. The enemy opened a brisk machine gun and rifle fire for a very short time on the barrier and then suddenly ceased. They used many flares. Their artillery fire was very brisk, after some delay in getting started: Retaliating on our front and support trenches in the locality. Before (about midnight) they retaliated as far back as the rear of hill 63.

Our...

Our casualties in the attacking party was only one man wounded.

The field gun was taken in during the night by the pave road past CHATEAU LA HUTTE by motor cars as far as the road junction at U.14 a, 5.4 and man handled from there down, the wheels being wrapped with old rubber tyres. It was placed on the road at the barrier and after firing about 20 rounds rapid (4 a.m.) it was quickly withdrawn in the same manner. Though several shells fell close to the gun and motors on its return it was not hit and there were no casualties to its crew at any time.

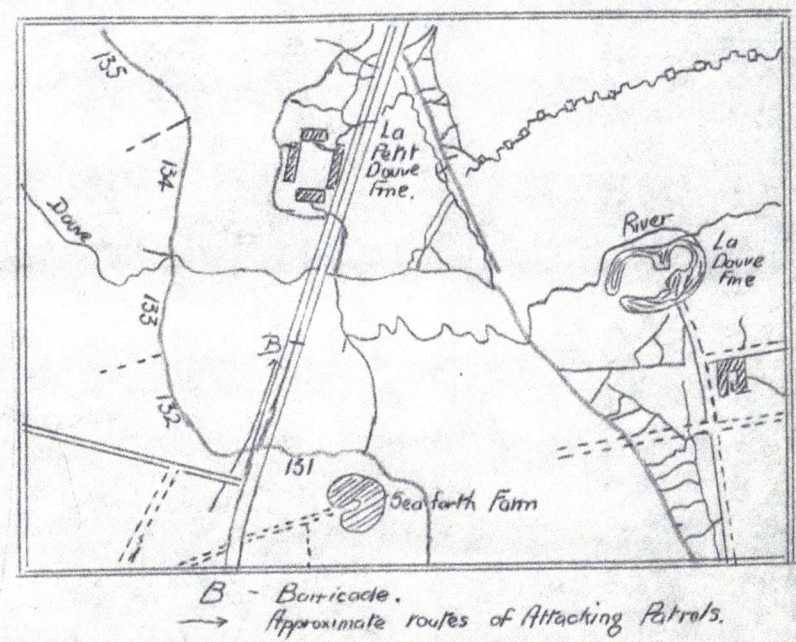

B - Barricade.
→ Approximate routes of Attacking Patrols.

LOCATION OF BARRIER CAPTURED BY 5th CANADIAN INF. BATTALION.

The barrier consisted of a large tree across the road with sandbags and a trench in the rear; there were dugouts alongside the whole connected into the ruins of a small brick house by the east side of the road.

An officer...

An officer and several men of 2nd Canadian Field Company accompanied the assaulting party to the barrier prepared for its demolition if required.

Our party remained in the enemy's barrier until daybreak and then withdrew to the sap-head alongside.

Report on Minor Enterprise carried out
by
8th Bn. Somerset L.I., 63rd Infantry Brigade.

Objects of Operation.

1. The enterprise was a "cutting out" expedition with the following objects:-

    (a) To kill as many Germans as possible.
    (b) To take some prisoners for identification.
    (c) To destroy a Mine Shaft, if found.
    (d) To ascertain whether arrangements for installing gas had been made.

2. <u>Strength of Force.</u>

    Previous reconnaissances had shown that the enemy's Sentries are not always on the alert.

    It was realized that this might mean that the Front Trenches were only lightly held, in which case a small force would have sufficed. However it was decided that the importance of maintaining the fighting spirit of the men was paramount and to make the strength of the attacking party as large as possible in consonance with the objects to be attained. The strength was limited to 120 men selected from volunteers.

3. <u>Selection of Objective.</u>

    It had been previously decided that the attack should be made from Trench 70 (The MUSHROOM).
    In order to justify the successful employment of as large force as contemplated in para 2 it was essential that

    (a) The attack should be a surprise.
    (b) The distance to be traversed should be as short as possible.
    (c) The portion of the enemy's line to be attacked

should, if possible, include a Main Communication Trench as this would probably ensure that the Trench at this point was held, and Officers Dug-outs and Machine Gun Emplacements might reasonably be expected to be found near this point.

Accordingly the portion of the enemy's line selected to be attacked was from I 11 c 5.2½ to I 11 c 6.6½ which included the main communication trench (SEARCHLIGHT STREET) at I 11 c 5.4½.

The disadvantages of this objective were:-

(a) The advance was completely enfiladed from the Railway Salient I 11 a 3.2

(b) No covered lines of approach were available.

4. <u>Preliminary Training and Preparations.</u>

The men selected for the enterprise were billeted together.

Trenches were dug according to scale to represent the German Trenches from I 11 c 6.6½ to I 11 c 5.2½ as taken from an aeroplane photograph.

The attack was practised by day and by night for three days, each man using the exact tools he would use in the actual attack. Consequently each man knew his place thoroughly, and the attack went like clockwork. The men practised the attack for the last time at 5 a.m. on the morning of the 15th. They then rested all day.

5. <u>Preliminary Reconnaissances.</u>

Previous Reconnaissances were carried out very thoroughly by Officers and the presence of a ditch believed to exist between the enemy's wire and parapet was confirmed.

Some chunks were cut out of the enemy's wire on Night of 13th.

The enemy's listening post was invariably found unoccupied.

6. **Artillery Preparation.**

A Preliminary Artillery Bombardment took place on December 8th and on December 15th a very complete Bombardment was carried out and the wire opposite point of attack was well cut in places sufficient allow the Infantry to pass through. As a measure precaution, mats were taken and these proved very useful to throw across the loose wire.

The O.C. Som L.I. spent the day with the F.O.O. and ched the bombardment of the enemy's machine gun emplacements and the wire cutting, taking note of t exact bearing to the best part made by "A" Battery through the enemy's wire. The enemy's wire was al cut in two other places.

7. **Narrative of Events December 16th.**

(a) Preliminary Reconnaissance.

At 12.15 a.m. 16th December a patrol was sent out under 2nd Lieut. Wallis to find out if enemy's listening post was occupied, and to see if enemy were on the alert. The Patrol spent twenty minutes at enemy's wire and were not fired at. They returned at 1.30 a.m. and reported listening post unoccupied, enemy not alert and sounds of whistling and talking coming from their trench.

(b) The Advance.

At 2.45 a.m. the concentration being complete the o was given for the Bridging Ladders and Mats to be taken over the parapet. This was done, and the men followed them, and lay down behind our knife rests in the correct order for the advance. At 3 a.m. the knife rests were noiselessly removed, and the signal given for the advance, which was carried out very quietly and slowly.

The officer leading the advance, took with him a roll of broad white ri one end of which was left in Bay 13, and moving on a bearing of 116 deg magnetic, unrolled the ribbon as he went, leaving behind a white path from our trenches to the point in the German Wire where the path had been cut. He passed the ribbon through the german wire and tied it beyond the wire. This ribbon was most effective as it ensured the men finding the best way through the enemy's wire and also the right way home again.

(c) Passage and Obstacles.

2nd Lieut Withers' Party was the first to reach the enemy's wire. They put down their mats over the broken knife rests, and the whole assaulting party then crossed the wire and ditch by the mats, without the slightest noise.

(d) Entry into German Trenches.

They then extended along the German Parapet and crawled up to the top of it, from whence 2nd Lieut Withers saw three men talking together in the trench. He shot one and jumped into the trench closely followed by the whole party. The other two men tried to run and were bayoneted. 2nd Lieut. Withers entered the German Trench at about 3.16 a.m. and the last man got in about 3.20 a.m., just as the guns commenced.

The enemy was completely surprised and the assaulting troops were into the trenches before any alarm was given, notwithstanding the fact that a few Very Lights were sent up close on our flanks, during the advance across NO MANS LAND.

The men were very steady, however, and remained motionless whenever a light was up.

A few of the enemy showed fight. Three men tried to rush Sergeant Coxen, but he shot two with his revolver and took the third man prisoner. The Officer would not surrender, and had to be shot.

Lieut.Shepherd R.E. searched for the Mine Shaft but could not find it, and so he exploded his charge in a Steel Machine Gun Emplacement.

One Machine Gun which was not even loaded was taken out of the trench but the men could not unfix it from its stand, and it was abandoned in the German Ditch, as it was extremely heavy and the mud was very deep, and the sides of the ditch very steep and slippery.

All removable articles were removed, all telephone wires cut, and some bombs were exploded in each dug-out on leaving them.

(e) <u>Withdrawal.</u> At 3.35 a.m. the signal for retirement was given, and the return to our trenches was all completed by 3.50 a.m. The whole enterprise was carried out without a single casualty. Later after returning to our trenches, the attacking force lost 3 killed and 7 wounded from hostile shell fire. Seven prisoners were captured and twenty killed. The remainder fled.

(f) The success of the enterprise was due to the splendid co-operation of all arms, particularly the Royal Artillery and the Royal Engineers. The mats made by Major Close R.E. for the purpose of getting over their wire answering the purpose entirely, and enabling the attacking force to reach the enemy's parapet <u>without notice</u>, and without cutting a single strand of wire with wire cutters. The men were very steady and never got out of hand. The men blackened their faces and wore Gas Helmets and this proved an easy mark of recognition.

8. German Trenches.

(a) The German Front Line Trench was in good condition, quite dry, well boarded and wired. There are no traverses but the trench is zig zag. The lateral communication trench is in a very bad condition and is knee deep in water, has no parados. Altogether their trenches are in no better condition than ours. The parapets are very high and their Front Line Trench not much below ground level which perhaps accounts for its dryness. The depth of the trench is estimated at 7 to 10 feet. Portions of the Firing Trench appear not to be provided with a continuous Fire Step. No sandbags are used for revetting the parapet, boards being employed for this purpose up to within 2 feet of top of parapet. The parados is about 4' 6" high and on further side of this parados the ground is quite open and exposed to fire and view from

Support Trench. The top of the interior slope of the
parapet is loose earth revetted with wire. No loop-holes
were noticed.

There were no signs whatever of any gas fixtures or
cyclinders, although a very sharp look-out was kept for
these.

(b) The enemy's trenches are not strongly held. The attack
embraced a front of about 150 yards of their trench but
only twenty of the enemy were killed, and about the same
number fled along the flanks and communication trenches
in front of our bombers, and were undoubtedly caught by
our shell fire there. This with the seven prisoners we
took, would appear to be all the men that were occupying
150 yards of front line trench.

9. Communications.

Communications were quickly established between the
German Trench and Trench 70, but the communciation to
Brigade Headquarters failed. Nine orderlies in all were
employed but all were either killed or wounded. Practically
from the beginning all the wires were cut except one
Artillery wire.

10. Hostile Retaliation.

Our enemy's machine gun opened fire but was quickly
silenced. There was very little hostile rifle fire but
the enemy retaliated very violently with Artillery, and
the MUSHROOM was heavily shelled, especially the flanks
and the communication trenches. The majority of the
casualties sustained were during this period of shelling
after our Infantry had returned to their trenches.

A hostile patrol of 4 or 5 men approached the
MUSHROOM about 4.30 a.m. apparently to see if it had
been abandoned, but quickly retired on being fired
upon.

11. The attack was carried out strictly in accordance with
the Battalion Operation Order issued and attached
as an Appendix.

Comments.

1. Use of Mine Galleries when available.

The presence of mind shown by Lieut.Shepherd R.E. who
brought back several men by the mining galleries
undoubtedly saved many lives.

2. Hour of Attack.

The time selected for the attack was purposely fixed
for an hour and a half after the moon had set as it was
thought that if the attack did not take place soon
after the moon had set, the enemy might relax their
vigilance.
In point of actual fact, this apparently did happen.
The night was very dark and wet and admirably suited
to an enterprise of this nature.

3. The plan of blackening faces and wearing smoke helmets
undoubtedly proved of great help in distinguishing
between friend and foe.

4. The white ribbon tape proved most useful in marking the route both to and from the enemy's trenches.

5. The great advantage of using rows of knife rests in front of our trenches is that gaps can be easily made by removing the knife rests when our Infantry take the offensive. This obviates the necessity of cutting our own wire beforehand and thus advertising the point from which our attack is to start.

6. It was noticed that during the process of wire cutting, the shrapnel which burst on graze underneath the wire was far more efficacious than shrapnel burst in the air.

BRIGADE ORDERS

BY

Brigadier General E.R.Hill,
Commanding 63rd Infantry Brigade.

App II

TUESDAY,
28th December 1915.

137. HONOURS AND AWARDS.

The following awards for gallantry in action are published for information :-

TO BE COMPANIONS OF THE DISTINGUISHED SERVICE ORDER.

Lieut-Colonel Louis Charles HOWARD.
8th Bn. Somerset Light Infantry.
(Since killed in action on night 23rd/24th Dec.1915 whilst reconnoitring in sap between the craters)

Enterprise night 15th/16th December 1915, East of ARMENTIERES.
From the moment he was told that this enterprise was to be entrusted to his Battalion, worked with the greatest energy to ensure its sucess. He inspired all ranks with his enthusiasm and confidence and the success of the Operation owes much to his example both before the day and on the Night of the enterprise when he organized the advance from and the retirement to the MUSHROOM, the latter under heavy shell fire with much skill and with complete indifference to personal danger.
He has been previously recommended for gallant work near LOOS on 26th September,1915.

Captain Richard Hall HUNTINGTON.
8th Bn. Somerset Light Infantry
Enterprise night 15th/16th December 1915, East of ARMENTIERES.
Was in Command of attacking party and carried it to a successful issue.

AWARDED THE MILITARY CROSS.

2nd Lieut. Frank Dean WITHERS.
8th Bn. Somerset Light Infantry.

Enterprise night 15th/16th December 1915, East of ARMENTIERES.
Was first into the German trenches and shot the sentry.

AWARDED THE DISTINGUISHED CONDUCT MEDAL.

No.15575 Sergt. John William COXON.
Enterprise night 15th/16th December 1915, East of ARMENTIERES.
Was attacked by three Germans in the German trenches. He killed two and took the other prisoner.

No.15802 Corpl. Andrew Lees FENWICK.
Enterprise night 15th/16th December 1915, East of ARMENTIERES.
Was first of the bombing party throughout the attack, also shewed great coolness and resource whilst on patrol duty night 13th/14th December, 1915.

No.12190 Private Frank Arthur JEFFERIES.
(Since killed in action on night 20th Dec 1915, when as a bomber he was protecting a working party on the mine crater and singlehanded attacked and drove off a German patrol, but was killed by another party of the enemy before he could return)
Enterprise night 15th/16th December 1915, East of ARMENTIERES.
Formed part of Bombing party and shewed great coolness and gallantry throughout the attack. Was recommended for D.C.M. for gallantry at CHALK PITS 26/9/15.

App III

(2)

HONOURS AND AWARDS (CONTD)

AWARDED THE DISTINGUISHED CONDUCT MEDAL. (Contd.)

No 15763 Sergeant John BLACK.
East of ARMENTIERES on the night 15/16th December 1915.
This N.C.O. was in charge of a bombing party and displayed great gallantry throughout the attack. On the morning of 19th December 1915 the Germans exploded a mine and delivered an attack. Sergt. Black displayed great presence of mind and courage in repelling them. On the night of 20/21st December 1915, the enemy made a bombing attack on the mine crater. Sergeant Black again displayed great gallantry and set a fine example to all. Although seriously wounded and in great pain he continued to give directions until he was carried away.

All 8th Bn. Somerset Light Infantry.

138. OFFICERS.

Unit to furnish Officers for Divisional Observation Station on Wednesday and Thursday 29th and 30th instant (vide Divisional Memorandum G.24) dated 6th December, 1915:-

4th Middlesex Regt.

139. COURT MARTIAL.

The detail of Officers mentioned below will assemble at the Headquarters of the 8th Somerset L.I. at 10.0 a.m. 28th inst., for the purpose of trying by Field General Court Martial No. 11/12150 Pte. J. Lynch and No. 10/15749 Pte. W. Fish, both of 10th Bn. York & Lancaster Regt., and any other persons as may be brought before them.

President   Major .... Mitchell,   4th ....
Members   Capt. .. Warrington,   8th Somerset L.I.
           Capt. .. ..,   8th Somerset L.I.

On excuse will be named and all ranks as required to attend. Proceedings will be forwarded to .... Stain, 63rd Infantry Brigade Headquarters.

A.K. Macdonald Major.
63rd Infantry Brigade.

5 R

Army Form C. 2118

WAR DIARY of 8th Battalion Somerset L.I.

INTELLIGENCE SUMMARY

January 1916.

(Erase heading not required.)

Instructions regarding War Diaries and Intelligence Summaries are contained in F.S. Regs., Part II. and the Staff Manual respectively. Title Pages will be prepared in manuscript.

Place	Date	Hour	Summary of Events and Information	Remarks and references to Appendices
ARMENTIERES.	Jan 1st 1916.		On the night of Dec. 31st – 1st Jan. Lieut R.E. Johnson rejoined from Base, and a draft of 20 N.C.O's and men also joined us from the 2nd Entrenching Battalion, they were provided with Iron Rations and Smoke Helmets.	
	2nd.		We went into the trenches from our billets on the evening of the 1st, and on the following day Lieut Lockwood left us, and proceeded to the 2nd Echelon, Base.	
	4th 5th		2nd Lieut Dowling reported his arrival on the 4th, and we came out of the trenches on the 5th. That day Capt Marsh was killed by a sniper about 3. P.M. at the junction of Trenches 69 & 70. 2nd Lieuts Adlam and Dowling reported their arrival on the 5th, and 2nd Lieut Dalrymple on the 7th.	
	8th		Capt Jollivet rejoined from Hospital on the 8th, but the following day Major Vinderwood went to Hospital. We returned to the trenches on the evening of the 9th, and on this occasion we were only in for three days, being relieved on the 12th by the 8th Lincolns, and not the 10th York & Lancs. The latter relieved the 4th Middlesex Regt, who had been holding trenches 67.68.69, which were south of the ones usually held by us.	
	12th		We were back in our rest billets from Jan 12-16th, and everything was very quiet except for about 20 shells which fell near the Hospice Mahieu	

Army Form C. 2118

Instructions regarding War Diaries and Intelligence Summaries are contained in F. S. Regs., Part II. and the Staff Manual respectively. Title Pages will be prepared in manuscript.

WAR DIARY of 8th Battalion Somerset L.I.

INTELLIGENCE SUMMARY

January 1916.

(Erase heading not required.)

Place	Date	Hour	Summary of Events and Information	Remarks and references to Appendices
ARMENTIERES	Jan 16th 1916.		On the evening of the 15th, this shelling caused us 70 casualties. On the evening of the 16th we took over trenches 67. 68. and 69 from the 10th York & Lancs. These trenches were considerably more comfortable than the one previously occupied by us. We were then on the extreme right of our Division, and the Battalion (12th & 13th Durham L.I. as the one might be) on our right belonged to the 23rd Division.	
	21st		After our usual spell of four days in the trenches we returned to our billets, and the following day, the 21st, Major J. W. Scott, on his return from leave in England, having reported his arrival to the Brigade, took over the command of this Battalion. A draft of 50 N.C.O's and men were sent to us from the 2nd Entrenching Battalion and joined us on the 26th.	
	26th			
	28th		We were in the trenches (67.68 & 69) from the 24th–28th, and on the afternoon of the 28th our trenches (chiefly 69, which was held by Capt Fluard's Company, "B" Co) were subjected to a very severe bombardment which lasted for about half an hour. Considering the intensity of the shelling, the damage done was remarkably slight, and our casualties were only seven wounded. We were relieved that same evening and returned to the Hospice Mahieu, where we now are.	

J W Scott Major
Cmdg 8 Som. L.I.

WAR DIARY

Army Form C. 2118

8th Battalion Somerset L.I.

INTELLIGENCE SUMMARY

Place	Date	Hour	Summary of Events and Information	Remarks and references to Appendices
ARMENTIERS	1.2.16		On the evening of 1st February we went into the trenches, and took over Trenches 70-73 inclusive from the 8th Lincolns. We remained in the firing line for four days which were very quiet, and, on a new system of holding the line being adopted, on the evening of the 5th	
	5.2.16		the 4th Middlesex took over Trenches 73 and 72, and the 8th Lincolns relieved us of Trenches 70 and 71. We were then acting as Brigade Reserve, and as such held the Subsidiary from FERME DE LA BUTTERNE to just south of the LILLE ROAD. We were there for two days, and then went relieved on the evening of the 7th by the 8th Lincolns, and then	
	7.2.16		returned to our usual billets (HOSPICE MAHIEU and Blue Factory) in the town.	
	9.2.16		On the 9th 2nd Lieut Withers was admitted to Field Ambulance, and on the same day 2nd Lieut Ball rejoined us from the Base. We went into the trenches on the early morning of the 14th	
	14.2.16		taking over Trenches 77-82 from the 15th Durham L.I. We were in the front line for 6 days and were relieved on the early morning	
	20.2.16		of the 20th by the 8th Lincolns. We were in Brigade Reserve for three days, and on the evening of the 23rd we relieved the 10th York and Lancs who were holding the subsidiary line from the PONT BALLOT Road to the River LYS.	

Army Form C. 2118

WAR DIARY
INTELLIGENCE SUMMARY
(Erase heading not required.)

Instructions regarding War Diaries and Intelligence Summaries are contained in F. S. Regs., Part II. and the Staff Manual respectively. Title Pages will be prepared in manuscript.

Place	Date	Hour	Summary of Events and Information	Remarks and references to Appendices
ARMENTIERES	25.2.16		The 13th Northumberland Fusiliers on the night of 25th – 26th, and not returned to our billets for 6 days. 2nd Lieut Stead went to Field ambulance on the 23rd.	App 1.
			2nd Lieut E.G. Shrine (attached 21st Trench Mortar Brigade) was awarded the Military Cross.	App. 2.
			No 7374 Pte Hughes R. was awarded the D.C.M.
			We were notified on the 26th that acting Qmr J.J. Schooling was appointed Qmr with honorary rank of Lieutenant.
			Capt Huntington was promoted temporary major, and 2nd Lieut W.S. Worden was promoted temporary Captain in the Gazette of Feb 26th

J. Scott Lt/Col
Comdy 8th Bn Lf

To Base Commandant
    E.A.D.
    —
I herewith return your
Z.E. 378 & 381 with many
thanks for kind loan
of them.

                J.H. Chapman
7-12-16
                MAJOR
            FIELD OFFICER i/c TRAINING
                ETAPLES

Appendix 1

Extract from Batt. Orders. Dated. 16.2.16.

495 The following decoration has been
awarded
(The Military Cross)
Second Lieut S.H. Skrine, 8th Batt
Somerst. Light Infantry (attached
21st Trench Mortar Brigade).

Certified true copy.
R.S.W. Barkworth
Lieut. & Som. L.I.

Appendix 2.

Extract from Batt. Orders. Dated. 22-2-16.

511 The following decoration has been
awarded.
(Distinguished Conduct Medal)
7374. Pte. Hughes. R.
8th Batt. Somerset. L.I. (Authority
London Gazette dated 14/1/16).

Certified true copy.
R. S. W. Horshenda
Lieut. 8-Som. L.I.

8 Somervel L.I.
Vol 7

WAR DIARY of 2nd Battalion Somerset L.I.

INTELLIGENCE SUMMARY

Army Form C. 2118

Place	Date 1916	Hour	Summary of Events and Information	Remarks and references to Appendices
ARMENTIERES	March 2nd		On the night of the 2nd-3rd we took over the Subsidiary Line from Lille Road to Rue de la Buterne from the 15th Durham L.I. We were there for three days, and on one occasion the left of our line was shelled rather heavily during the morning. We were relieved on the evening of the 5th by the 10th York and Lancs, and returned to our billets in the town for three days.	
	5th		On the 2nd of March 2nd Lieut Dowling was admitted to Field ambulance, and on the 5th Capt Schlesinger rejoined the Batt. from England, and 2nd Lieut Withers rejoined us from hospital	
	8th		On the evening of the 8th we went back to the front line trenches, and took over trenches 73-77 inclusive from the 4th Middlesex Regt. We were there for six days which were fairly quiet, except the last day, when the left & and centre of our line was severely shelled : our casualties were two killed and two wounded.	
	14th		The 10th York and Lancs relieved us on the night of the 14th-15th, and we returned to ARMENTIERES, the whole Battalion being billeted this time in the Hospice Civil, Rue de Retours	

Army Form C. 2118

WAR DIARY

of 8th Battalion

INTELLIGENCE SUMMARY Somerset L.I.

(Erase heading not required.)

Place	Date	Hour	Summary of Events and Information	Remarks and references to Appendices
ARMENTIERES	1916 March 20th		We were in billets in ARMENTIERES for six days, and then, our Division being relieved by the 17th Division, we marched on the 20th to STEENTJE having been in that district for nearly five months. The following day we marched to STRAZEELE.	
STEENTJE	20th			
STRAZEELE	21st			
	24th		On the 24th 2nd Lieuts Ham and Mellor joined the Battalion and on the 28th Capt and Adjt A.W. Phillips left us to join the staff at the 2nd Army School of Instruction.	
			During our time at STRAZEELE, which lasted until the end of the month, we carried out usual training in A.Co's.	
	29th		On the 29th we marched past General Plumer (G.O.C. 2nd Army) and General Ferguson (G.O.C. 2nd Corps), both of whom congratulated the Battalion on its smart turnout. General Ferguson also wished his thanks to be conveyed to the men for the good work that they had done in the trenches during the winter.	

[signature]
Comdg 8th Somerset L.I.

WAR DIARY of 8th (S) Battalion XXI Somerset L.I. Vol 8

INTELLIGENCE SUMMARY

Army Form C. 2118

Place	Date	Hour	Summary of Events and Information	Remarks and references to Appendices
STRAZEELE	April 1st 1916		On the early morning of April 1st, the Battalion left the STRAZEELE area. We entrained at GODEWAERSVELDE, and arrived at LONGEAU near AMIENS about 2 p.m. We detrained there and marched to ALLONVILLE, where we remained until the 7th.	
ALLONVILLE	7.4.16		On the 7th April we carried out usual training.	
VILLE	7.4.16		We marched to VILLE, but we only remained there a short time as on the 9th we moved on to the village of MEAULT.	
MEAULT	9.4.16		Lieut Pike went to hospital on the 9th and returned on the 14th; 2nd Lieut KELLETT joined us on the 14th, and 2nd Lt SAUNDERS went to hospital on the 15th. On the morning of the 14th we were inspected by G.O.C. 21st Division, and that afternoon we went into the trenches for the first time in this district, relieving the 1st Batt Yorks Regt. On our left was a Batt of the 4th MIDDLESEX. The trenches which we were holding were about a mile north west of FRICOURT Village. During this tour in the trenches we only had four casualties, two killed and two wounded. We were relieved on the evening of the 23rd	
	23.4.16			

Army Form C. 2118

WAR DIARY
of 8th (S) Battalion Somerset L.I.
INTELLIGENCE SUMMARY

Instructions regarding War Diaries and Intelligence Summaries are contained in F. S. Regs., Part II. and the Staff Manual respectively. Title Pages will be prepared in manuscript.

(Erase heading not required.)

Place	Date	Hour	Summary of Events and Information	Remarks and references to Appendices
BUIRE LA NEUVILLE	23.4.16		by the 10th Yorks. The night of the 23rd we spent in billets at BUIRE, and the following day the Battalion marched to LA NEUVILLE. Capt Slade Wright went to hospital on the 22nd and referred on the 27th, and Col Scott went to hospital on the 26th, but referred on the 28th.	
	30.4.16		We are at present still at LA NEUVILLE, and are carrying out usual training.	

J.S. Scott Lt Col.

WAR DIARY of 8th (S) Batt. Somerset L.I.

INTELLIGENCE SUMMARY

Army Form C. 2118
Vol 9

Place	Date	Hour	Summary of Events and Information	Remarks and references to Appendices
LA NEUVILLE	2.5.16		On the 2nd May Major R.L. Huntington went to Field Ambulance. On the 3rd May the Batt. marched to BUIRE, where we were billeted for ten days, during this time the whole Batt. was employed on working parties.	
BUIRE	3.5.16		2nd Lt Maurice went to Field Ambulance.	
	5.5.16		Lieut W.C. Whiting joined the Batt. on the 6th. 2nd Lt Young returned from hospital on the 8th, and on the same day 2nd Lt Morgan went to Field Ambulance.	
	8.6.16			
	12.5.16		Major Huntington returned from Field Ambulance on the 12th, and on the afternoon of that day the Batt. took over the left sector of the trenches from the 10th K.O.Y.L.I. On the night of the 13th–14th of May the Batt. was detailed to attempt a cutting out expedition. Capt Feliot was in charge of the party which consisted of 70 officers, N.C.O's and men. 2nd Lt Withers was in charge of a small advance party whose duty was to lay an explosive charge in the barbed wire in front of the German trenches. After some delay the charge was fired and the whole party rushed forward. The outer wire had been destroyed, but at the	

Army Form C. 2118

WAR DIARY of 8th (S) Batt
INTELLIGENCE SUMMARY Somerset L.I.

(Erase heading not required.)

Instructions regarding War Diaries and Intelligence Summaries are contained in F. S. Regs., Part II. and the Staff Manual respectively. Title Pages will be prepared in manuscript.

Place	Date	Hour	Summary of Events and Information	Remarks and references to Appendices
			bottom of the German trench there was some uncut wire and also some knife rests. 2nd Lieut Vernon and the leading men tried to force their way through the wire, but were unsuccessful. Our bombers were now throwing bombs, and, as the enemy began to retaliate, the order was given to retire. The casualties were 2nd Lt Vernon and one N.C.O. killed, and Capt Jebet wounded. Capt Jebet had got caught up in the barbed wire and so was a minute or two behind the party in getting back. 2nd Lt Vernon was seen back on our parapet by several of the party, and it is very probable that when he heard a report that Capt Jebet had not returned, he went out to look for him, as he was killed close to the German wire, but some little distance off the original line of advance.	
	14·5·16		On the following night Sgt Fenwick J.C.M. was killed by a bullet, and on the 15th we were relieved in the front line by the 10th York and Lancs.	
	15·5·16		The Batt. were billeted in MEAULTE till the night of the	

Army Form C. 2118

WAR DIARY of 8th (S) Batt.
INTELLIGENCE SUMMARY Somerset L.I.

(Erase heading not required.)

Instructions regarding War Diaries and Intelligence
Summaries are contained in F. S. Regs., Part II.
and the Staff Manual respectively. Title Pages
will be prepared in manuscript.

Place	Date	Hour	Summary of Events and Information	Remarks and references to Appendices
LA NEUVILLE	22.5.16		22nd – 23rd when the marched back to LA NEUVILLE, where we were billeted for ten days and carried out usual training. 2nd Lieuts Busby, Hinton and Sheatley joined the Batt. on the 23rd, 2nd Lieuts Allott, Lewis, W.H. Baker and Webb on the 24th, and 2nd Lt Chalmers on the 27th. The G.O.C. Division inspected the Batt. on the morning of the 31st. The Battalion was mentioned among other units in Sir Douglas Haig's first despatch dated 19th May 1916, for "specially good work while in the trenches in carrying out or repelling local attacks and raids."	

J. L. __ Lt Col
Comdg 8 Som L.I.

War Diary

of

8th Somerset Light Infantry.

for

June & July 1916

Army Form C. 2118

WAR DIARY or INTELLIGENCE SUMMARY
(Erase heading not required.)

21/7/63 STAFF Somerset L.I. JUNE–JULY 1916 Somerset
63/34 21/8

Vols 10. 11

Place	Date	Hour	Summary of Events and Information	Remarks and references to Appendices
LA NEUVILLE	2.6.16		The 8/Som.L.I marched from LA NEUVILLE to VILLE where he was billeted for 10 days. During this period men employed on working parties.	
VILLE	11.6.16		The Batt - went into the trenches, taking over left sector of Fricourt front. During this period on casualties were, killed 4 wounded OR	
	15.6.16		The Batt - was relieved by the 10'6" York & Lancs & held the intermediary line for 5 days. 10'6" Batt - H.Q at MEAULTE. A draft of 86 men arrived on 7.6.16 - another of 55 men on the 19th. Lt. R.H.G. Bailey went to First Ambulance on the 13th. 2d Lt. Barker joined the Batt on the 17th. Lt. G.H. Smithers rejoined from 62nd T.M. Battery on 19th.	
LA NEUVILLE	20.6.16		The Batt - marched to LA NEUVILLE - short parade was held daily & the men were practised in "getting in & out of trenches". Bde Sports were held in the afternoon of 24.6.16	
" "	25.6.16		Capt. M.A.H. Campbell joined from (1st 13th)	
	26.6.16		The Batt - marched from LA NEUVILLE to VILLE	
VILLE	27.6.16		The Batt - marched from VILLE to the trenches & took over the assembly trenches + MARISCHAL St. and STONEHAVEN St. from R.d. MIDDLESEX. The attack having been put off 48hrs we took up & kept 6 men in the retirs.	
Trenches	28.6.16		In the evening we took over from Rd. MIDDLESEX. The Bombardment of the Enemys position commenced 26.6.16 & kept up till 1.7.16	

102

Place	Date	Hour	Summary of Events and Information	Remarks and references to Appendices
TRENCHES.	29.6.16		Held front line — The 4th Middlesex returned to their original position, we took over the firing line which had been vacated at 9 only just opened at the top. Bn. HQrs. moved up to SHUTTLE LANE at 9.30 p.m. The night was employed in renewing our front line wire & preparing for assault. At 6.30 a.m. trench ladders were put in place and took an intense Artillery	
"	1.7.16		barrage was opened.	
		7.30 AM	was ZERO time for assault at 7.	
		7.25 AM	first waves of B & C Coys crawled out. The Battalion was ordered to attack in the following formation "B" & C Coys in front "B" on right "C" on left were to advance in 4 lines of Platoons at 2 paces interval. Supports about 100 x between lines — Supported by "A" Coy in 2 lines of 2 Coys. "D" Coy coming on in rear in Artillery formation. E.G. in lines of platoons in file as a carrying party for S.A.A. - Bombs - picks + shovels - Trench stores etc. Directly the Artillery barrage lifted our men advanced in great time. They were met by very heavy machine gun + rifle fire and although	

WAR DIARY
or
INTELLIGENCE SUMMARY
(Erase heading not required.)

Army Form C. 2118

Place	Date	Hour	Summary of Events and Information	Remarks and references to Appendices
			Officers & men were being hit & falling everywhere the advance went steadily on, and was reported to by a Brigade Major who witnessed it to have been magnificent. The leading platoons lost quite 50% going across "No Mans Land". On arrival near the enemys front line they were momentarily held up by a machine gun, but they on the sweepers supporting them came up & they soon got in. Already the enemy had opened an Artillery Barrage on "No Mans Land" & our front line trench - which caused heavy casualties among the supports. The only enemy found alive in this front line were a few machine gunners, who were immediately killed. Our men worked their way down the German Communication Trench Bombing Dugouts which contained his Germans; there on 6 When the trenches had been battered out of all recognition, and only	

WAR DIARY or INTELLIGENCE SUMMARY

Army Form C. 2118

Place	Date	Hour	Summary of Events and Information	Remarks and references to Appendices
			Consisted of a heap of craters. They were supported by one STOKES gun but the Officer in charge + the team were soon knocked out; then a Lewis gun team of ours got up 4 but considerable help; machine gun men to make a further advance. This party was under Lt Kellett and worked its way from crater to crater until it got to LOZENGE ALLEY which had not been staffed by our Artillery, here they consolidated - making his stop the keener it was only a communication trench. The enemy's barrage of shrapnel prevented further advance. In LOZENGE ALLEY KELLETT's party joined up with Lt. A.H. HALL's party making a total of about 100, who had been doing much the same work - They held their position all night - during which time they repulsed a bombing attack coming from the direction of FRICOURT.	
	2.7.16	8.00 am	Capt. MAXWELL arrived with a party of reinforcements carrying rations; he had previously found Lt. AKROHYD, I.P. and about 30 men in BRANDY TRENCH wounded and given them rations	

WAR DIARY
or
INTELLIGENCE SUMMARY

(Erase heading not required.)

Army Form C. 2118

Place	Date	Hour	Summary of Events and Information	Remarks and references to Appendix.
	2.7.16	11.00 A.M.	Major R.H. Huntington's whereabouts were located & his party to of reinforcements carrying rations were guided down to Meuntenant Lozenge Alley. The following Officers joined with Maj Huntington :- Lt. S. Baker & Lt. Symins. During the morning a counter attack was expected from Fricourt and orders were received to be prepared for an attack from either direction. He arranged the trench accordingly and remained in the same position all night. Day and throughout the night of the 2nd. The following Officer reinforcements arrived Lt. F.J. Allam Lt. J.A. Ham and Lt. S.A.M. Dobson. 2/Lt Allam was ordered to take command of A Coy 2Lt. S. Baker " " " " B Coy Lt. R. Kellett " " " " C " Lt. J.A. Ham " " " " D " 2/Lt S.A.M. Dobson was attached to D Coy 2Lt Hall acted as Temporary Adjutant.	
Height of	2/3			

Place	Date	Hour	Summary of Events and Information	Remarks and references to Appendices
Lozenge Alley	3.7.16	About 9:00 am	2/Lt. AKERMAN and his party, have orders to remain where they were in BRANDY TRENCH as there was no more room in LOZENGE ALLEY. During the morning of the 3rd an attack was to be launched from CRUCIFIX TRENCH on to the line SHELTER WOOD – BOTTOM WOOD – and Capt. M.A. McCampbell, 2/Lt. S. BAKER and 2/Lt. G.A. Ham went to reconnoitre with a view to occupying CRUCIFIX Trench in support of the attack as soon as the attackers left it. The Battn. has not orders to take up this position. About 2 pm a senior officer was sent for by Bde H.Q. Capt. Campbell was sent, he was given instructions to reconnoitre PATCH ALLEY and if it was unoccupied to turn the 8/Somerset L.I. up there as Aeroplanes had reported enemy columns marching SW towards ROUND WOOD and a counter attack was expected, the 8/Somerset were to support the 6 2nd Bde, this turn has been completed about 5:0 pm Capt. Campbell was also ordered to reconnoitre WILLOW PATCH & SOUTH SAUSAGE Support — SODA Trench to junction of ROUND WOOD ALLEY	

Army Form C. 2118

WAR DIARY or **INTELLIGENCE SUMMARY**
(Erase heading not required.)

Instructions regarding War Diaries and Intelligence Summaries are contained in F.S. Regs., Part II. and the Staff Manual respectively. Title Pages will be prepared in manuscript.

Place	Date	Hour	Summary of Events and Information	Remarks and references to Appendices
Milly-sur-Somme	4.7.16	noon	to see if it was occupied by enemy and if so join up with 64th Bde on our left near WILLOW PATCH — The 64th Bde were found in position and no enemy encountered. The S/Sooth. J remained in their position until the early hours of the morning of 4-7-16 when we were relieved by a Company of the 12th Manchester Regt. We were ordered to march to DERNANCOURT and entrain — route via HAPPY VALLEY and MEAULTE. We reached DERNANCOURT about 10.0 Am	64th Bde
Bertangles	5.7.16		Arrived and detrained about noon — The Battn marched to VAUX	
	6.7.16		The Battn moved bilets and marched to BERTANGLES	
			The 63rd Bde was transferred from 21st to 37th Division.	
TALMAS	7.7.16		The Battn marched to TALMAS	
HALLOY	8.7.16		The Battn marched to HALLOY	
	10.7.16		Officers reconnoitred trenches front E of HANNESCAMP.	

1875. Wt. W593/826 1,000,000 4/15 J.B.C. & A. A.D.S.S./Forms/C. 2118.

Army Form C. 2118

WAR DIARY
or
INTELLIGENCE SUMMARY
(Erase heading not required.)

Place	Date	Hour	Summary of Events and Information	Remarks and references to Appendices
Hannescamp	11.7.16		Marched to HANNESCAMP and took over trenches from 47th Divn.	
Night	11/12		An enemy patrol attacked one of our posts in a sap head killing 1 and wounded 3 men.	
	14.7.16		Battn. was relieved in the trenches by the 9th London and marched back to HUMBERCAMP. The 3/4th Bn. had today been transferred to IV Corps.	
	15.7.16		Battn. marched to HOUVIN HOUVIGNEUR.	
	16.7.16		Battn. marched to VILLERS BRULIN.	
	18.7.16 to 25.7.16		to GOUY SERVINS. Major Huntington sick to hospital. "CAMBLAIN L'ABBE." Working parties were provided for the [enemy] from BERTHONVAL.	
	26.7.16		2nd Lieut. P. Hayes & T.L. Snow joined the Battn.	
	28.7.16		Capt. H. Harvey, 2nd Lieuts. L.S. Holmes, F.H.T. Jocelyne, E.A. Matthews, A. Garrard, W.R.B. Peel, R.S. Bryant, J.H.M. Hardyman, F.H. Baker, E.H. Morgan, H.J. Tucker, joined the battalion. Capt. S. Baker went sick.	
	30.7.16			
	31.7.16		Battn. relieved 8th London Regt. in BERTHONVAL I front line.	

Neil A. Stewart Major
Comdg 1/5 Somerset L.I.

www.ingramcontent.com/pod-product-compliance
Lightning Source LLC
Chambersburg PA
CBHW081238170426
43191CB00034B/1966